www.marcelolive.com

Rita is a fictional character inspired by a real Shetland pony that sometimes escapes from her field in pursuit of new adventures. She works at Park Lane Stables RDA, an award-winning RDA (Riding for the Disabled Association) centre with a wide programme of activities, including assisted riding, horse care, carriage driving, equine therapy and hippotherapy. This centre helps thousands of people every year with the help of horses and volunteers. Help their activity: https://www.parklanestables.co.uk/donate

ISBN: 9798333659231

The real Rita, eagerly waiting to return to the field after coming back from an adventure.

BOOK 1

Rita the Pony Explorer

Discovering the Secret Spot
The Adventure Begins

Rita the Explorer is a small, black Shetland pony with a big, white patch on her back. She lives in a beautiful paddock paradise with other horses.

They work at a special stable, helping people with special skills. When they are not working they rest, play and enjoy the sunshine in the field.

Rita loves her home and all her friends.

There's Max, a big, gentle horse
who loves to tell stories.

Tella is a graceful mare who always knows the best places to find helpful plants at the edges.

Then there's Rocky, a cheeky pony who loves to play tricks and make everyone laugh.

Rita loves her friends, but she is always curious about what lies beyond their land. She wonders what new adventures she might find if she could explore the world outside, even though she loves her home.

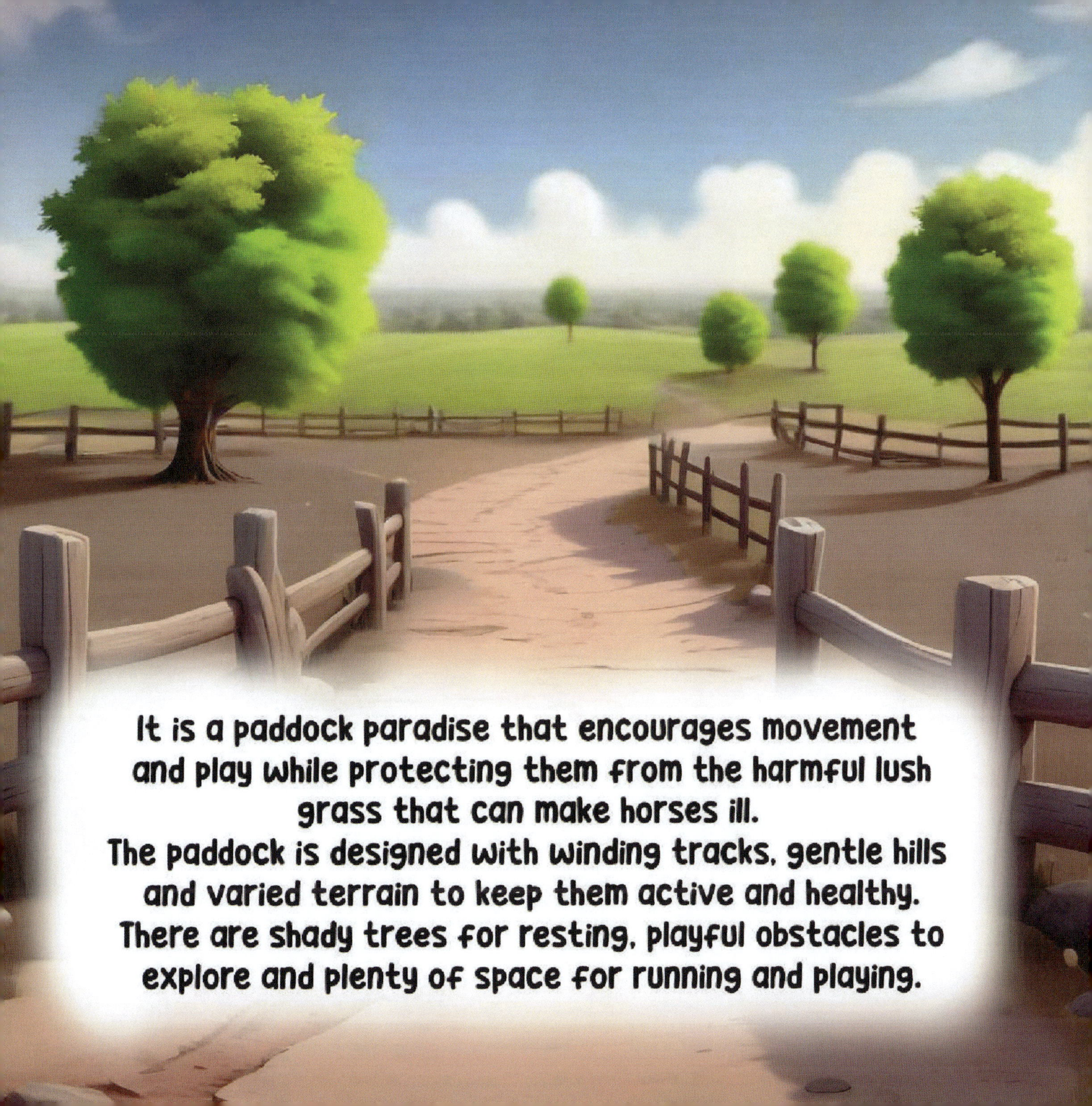

It is a paddock paradise that encourages movement and play while protecting them from the harmful lush grass that can make horses ill.
The paddock is designed with winding tracks, gentle hills and varied terrain to keep them active and healthy. There are shady trees for resting, playful obstacles to explore and plenty of space for running and playing.

One sunny morning, Rita decides to take a walk around the field. She trots along the fence, her nose twitching with excitement as she sniffs the fresh air. Birds sing in the trees, and butterflies dance around the flowers.

"Wow," she thinks. "I think I found a secret spot in the fence!"

Rita looks around to make sure no one is watching.
She pushes the board again and it moves a bit more.

she can see a path leading away from the field. The path is lined with tall trees and colourful flowers. It looks so inviting!

Rita's mind fills with thoughts of what might be out there. She imagines meeting new animal friends, finding hidden treasures and discovering magical places. But then she remembers her friends in the field and all the fun they have together.

With a sigh, Rita steps back from the fence. She knows she isn't ready to leave just yet. But now, she has something exciting to think about.

She can hardly wait to tell Max, Tella, and Rocky about her discovery.

As she trots back to her friends, Rita feels a mix of excitement and curiosity. She knows that one day, she will be brave enough to explore beyond the field.

But for now, she is happy to dream about the adventures that await her.

When she reaches her friends, Rita tells them all about the secret spot in the fence.

Rocky listen with wide eyes and big smiles.
They all agree that it sounds very exciting.

"We'll be here whenever you're ready, Rita," Max says kindly.

"Yes and maybe one day, we can all go on an adventure together!" Tella adds.

Rita nods, feeling happy and content. She knows that with friends like these, she can do anything.

And who knows? Maybe her next adventure is just around the corner.

And so, Rita the Explorer continues to play and learn with her friends, always keeping the secret spot in the fence in the back of her mind, dreaming of the day she'll be ready to explore the world beyond.

About the Author:

Marcel Olivé is a distinguished author and expert in Natural Horsemanship, as well as a horse and hoof care specialist.

With a deep passion for equine well-being, Marcel integrates horses into his practice as an Equine Assisted Facilitator and Leadership and Performance Coach. His extensive knowledge and transformational approaches have made him a respected figure in the equestrian community, where he continues to inspire and educate through his writing and hands-on work with both horses and humans.

Printed in Great Britain
by Amazon

57296994R00016